Book 1

Literature & Comprehension

Writing Skills

Language Arts
Activity Book

W9-CEK-675

K12

Book Staff and Contributors

Beth Zemble   *Director, Alternative Learning Strategies; Director, English Language Arts*
Marianne Murphy   *Senior Content Specialist*
Amy Rauen   *Senior Instructional Designer*
Miriam Greenwald, Mariana Holliday, Lenna King, David Shireman   *Instructional Designers*
Mary Beck Desmond   *Senior Text Editor*
Anne Vogel   *Text Editor*
Suzanne Montazer   *Creative Director, Print and ePublishing*
Jayoung Cho   *Senior Print Visual Designer*
Carol Leigh   *Print Visual Designer*
Stephanie Shaw Williams   *Cover Designer*
Anna Day   *Director, Instructional Design for Language Arts and History/Social Studies*
Joshua Briggs, Tim Mansfield, Lisa Moran   *Writers*
Amy Eward   *Senior Manager, Writers*
Susan Raley   *Senior Manager, Editors*
Alden Davidson   *Senior Project Manager*
David Johnson   *Director, Program Management Grades K–8*

Maria Szalay   *Executive Vice President, Product Development*
John Holdren   *Senior Vice President, Content and Curriculum*
David Pelizzari   *Vice President, K^{12} Content*
Kim Barcas   *Vice President, Creative*
Laura Seuschek   *Vice President, Assessment and Research*
Christopher Frescholtz   *Senior Director, Program Management*

Lisa Dimaio Iekel   *Director, Print Production and Manufacturing*
Ray Traugott   *Production Manager*

Credits

About K12 Inc.

K12 Inc. (NYSE: LRN) drives innovation and advances the quality of education by delivering state-of-the-art digital learning platforms and technology to students and school districts around the world. K12 is a company of educators offering its online and blended curriculum to charter schools, public school districts, private schools, and directly to families. More information can be found at K12.com.

978-1-60153-299-2
Printed by LSC Communications, Menasha, WI, USA, May 2019.

Contents

Literature & Comprehension

Writing Skills

Sentences

Paragraphs

Turn a Persuasive Essay into a Business Letter

Literature & Comprehension

Explore "The Wind and the Sun"

All About "The Wind and the Sun"

Fill in the boxes with plot events from the story in sequence. Then state the moral of the story.

At the beginning of the story,

In the middle of the story,

At the end of the story,

The moral of the story is _____

_____ .

Explore "The Bundle of Sticks"
All About "The Bundle Sticks"

Fill in the boxes with plot events from the story in sequence. Then state the moral of the story.

First,

Next,

Then,

Finally,

The moral of the story is _____

_____.

Explore "Why the Larks Flew Away"
All About "Why the Larks Flew Away"

Using a signal word to show order for each event, fill in the boxes with events from the story in sequence. Then state the moral of the story.

The moral of the story is _____

_____.

Reflections on Lessons Learned
Write a Summary of a Fable

Write a summary of the "The Wind and the Sun" or "The Bundle of Sticks." Follow this checklist as you write your summary.

☐ My summary has a beginning that includes

- title
- author, if there is one
- setting
- main characters

☐ My summary has a middle part that

- Tells three or more main events in sequence.
- Uses signal words such as *first*, *next*, *then*, and *finally*.

☐ My summary has a conclusion that tells the moral of the story.

☐ I've checked my writing for correct punctuation and spelling.

_____

_____

_____

_____

_____

_____

_____

_____

_____

_____

_____

_____

_____

_____

_____

_____

_____

_____

Explore "Chipmunk and Bear"
The Lesson in "Chipmunk and Bear"

Answer the questions. Write in complete sentences.

1. Chipmunk is clever. What is the result of his trick?

_____

_____

_____

_____

_____

_____

2. Explain how Chipmunk's tricks cause him problems.

_____

_____

_____

_____

_____

_____

_____

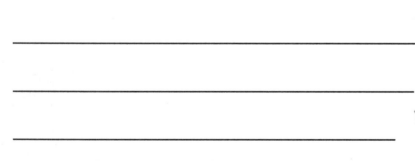

LITERATURE & COMPREHENSION

3. What do you think is the lesson of this folktale?

_____

_____

_____

_____

_____

_____

4. Chipmunk has the marks of his encounter with Bear on his back. Why might the marks on his back be a good lesson for Chipmunk and readers?

_____

_____

_____

_____

_____

_____

Explore "The Tiger, the Brahman, and the Jackal"

The Lesson in "The Tiger, the Brahman, and the Jackal"

Answer the questions. Write in complete sentences.

1. The Brahman and tiger cause some of their own problems. How?

   _____

   _____

   _____

   _____

   _____

   _____

2. The tiger and jackal both use a clever trick to solve their problems, but the tiger does not succeed in the end. Why?

   _____

   _____

   _____

   _____

   _____

3. What is the lesson of this folktale?

    _____

    _____

    _____

4. The tree, buffalo, and road say that the Brahman cannot expect
    kindness in return for kindness. Do you agree? Why or why not? Use
    examples from the story, other stories, and your own life to support
    your answer.

    _____

    _____

    _____

5. Imagine that the jackal had not come along in the story. If you were
    the Brahman, would you solve your problem with strength, cleverness,
    or in some other way? What would you do and why?

    _____

    _____

    _____

    _____

    _____

Explore "Squirrel and Spider"
The Lesson in "Squirrel and Spider"

Answer the questions. Write in complete sentences.

1. How are Spider and Crow alike?

   _____

   _____

2. Do you feel the same about Spider as you feel about Crow? Why or why not? Use examples from the story to support your answer.

   _____

   _____

   _____

3. What does the reader learn from Spider's experience?

   _____

   _____

   _____

4. Read the last paragraph of the story. What is this folktale's lesson?

   _____

   _____

   _____

5. Is it fair that Squirrel's problem is never solved? Why or why not?

_____

_____

_____

_____

6. Is it fair that Spider's problem is not solved? Why or why not?

_____

_____

_____

_____

7. What advice would you give Squirrel to solve his problem? Would you suggest strength or cleverness? Why?

_____

_____

_____

_____

Reflections on Animal Tales
Compare and Contrast Characters

Choose three characters from the three folktales: one that is honest and two that are tricky. Complete the Venn diagram to compare and contrast the three characters.

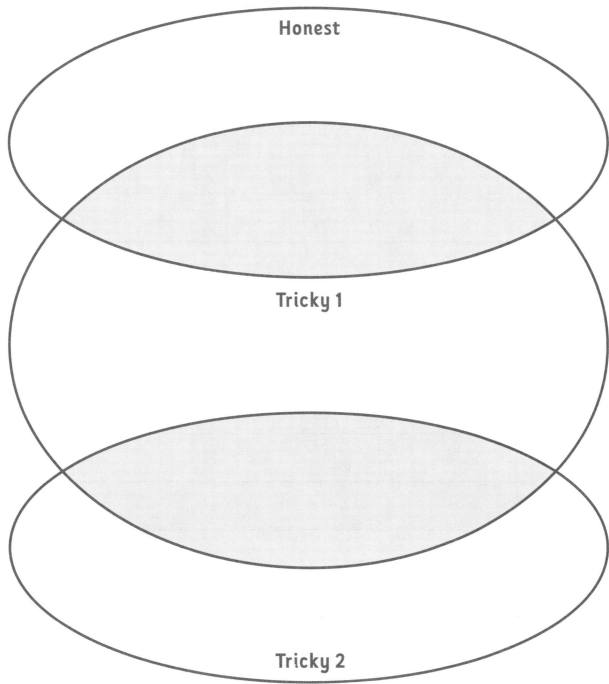

Honest

Tricky 1

Tricky 2

Write a paragraph about the lesson readers can learn from the three characters you chose. With your diagram to help you, follow this checklist as you write a paragaraph.

- First, introduce each character and tell which story each is from.
- Next, describe how the honest character tries to solve a problem and whether he succeeds.
- Then, describe how the first tricky character tries to solve a problem and whether he succeeds.
- Then, describe how the second tricky character tries to solve a problem and whether he succeeds.
- Finally, tell which character is best at solving problems and explain the lesson readers can learn from these characters' stories.

_____

_____

_____

_____

_____

_____

_____

_____

_____

_____

Explore "Charlie and Topsy"
How Does Charlie Change?

Answer the questions. Write in complete sentences.

1. Describe Charlie at the beginning of the story.
   Give examples from the story to support your answer.

   _____

   _____

   _____

2. What happens to Charlie in the middle of the story?
   Summarize what happens.

   _____

   _____

   _____

   _____

3. How does Charlie change because of what happens to him?
   Give examples from the story to support your answer.

   _____

   _____

   _____

4. How is meeting the giant girl good for Charlie?

_____

_____

_____

_____

_____

5. Why is it important to treat friends (including our animal friends) the way they would like to be treated? What happens when we don't?

_____

_____

_____

_____

_____

6. What is the lesson or theme of this story?

_____

_____

_____

_____

_____

LITERATURE & COMPREHENSION

Explore "Moufflu"
Explore Language and Theme

Read this passage from "Moufflu." Think about the words that help you form a mental picture or show how Moufflu and Lolo feel. Answer the questions. Write in complete sentences.

> When everyone was beginning to think that Lolo would never get better, Moufflu came back. Thin and dirty and caked with mud, he came dashing up the stairs one night at sunset. He was just as happy to see them as they were to see him. It seemed as if he would knock himself over wagging his tail.
>
> From that hour, Lolo began to get better. He would hardly let the dog out of his sight.

1. How does the author's language help create an image in the reader's mind of Lolo and Moufflu?

_____

_____

_____

_____

_____

_____

2. What does the author's language show us about the love between Moufflu and Lolo?

_____

_____

_____

_____

3. Moufflu comes home alone all the way from Rome. Lolo is very sick, but he gets better once Moufflu gets back. What does their love for each other help them do?

_____

_____

_____

4. What do you think is the theme of the story? Write your answer in a complete sentence.

_____

_____

_____

_____

Explore "Black Beauty"
Write as Black Beauty

Imagine that Black Beauty has a new challenge to face. He is sold to a new master who is cruel. The new master makes Black Beauty work very hard pulling heavy loads, and he whips the horse and won't let him rest. He doesn't give Black Beauty enough food, water, or warm blankets.

Write a paragraph from Black Beauty's perspective. Use the first-person point of view to tell how he feels about life with his new master. Think about Black Beauty's character traits and describe what he might do or think in this situation.

LITERATURE & COMPREHENSION

_____

_____

_____

_____

_____

_____

_____

_____

_____

_____

_____

_____

Reflections on Animals and Their People
Tell Moufflu's Side of the Story

Pretend that you are Moufflu, and retell the story from Moufflu's point of view. Organize your story this way:

- First, tell who you are and where you live. Be sure to explain how you feel about Lolo.

- Then, summarize what happens from the point at which the gentleman buys you until you return to Lolo. Use language that shows, rather than tells, when you say what happens to you and how you feel.

- Finally, end your story by telling how you feel about being home.

When you have finished your first draft, use this checklist to review your work. After you revise your story, write a neat final copy ready to publish and share.

☐ Tell the story with Moufflu as the first-person narrator. Use the words *I*, *me*, and *mine*.

☐ Describe events the way Moufflu would see them and feel about them. Stay true to his character traits.

☐ Be creative when describing Moufflu's journey home. Add details about new settings and what might have happened to him.

☐ Use showing language and vivid words to describe settings, events, characters, and Moufflu's feelings.

☐ Use order words and transition words to connect your sentences, ideas, and events.

☐ Tell what Moufflu says or thinks, what he does, and what others say about him to help readers understand Moufflu's character.

Write your first draft on this page.

_____

_____

_____

_____

_____

_____

_____

_____

_____

_____

_____

_____

Write your neat final copy on this page.

LITERATURE & COMPREHENSION

Explore "Forecasting the Weather"
Main Idea, Details, and Author's Purpose

Answer the questions in complete sentences. Use examples from the article to support your answers.

1. What are the headings of the four sidebars in the article "Forecasting the Weather"?

   _____

   _____

   _____

   _____

   _____

   _____

2. Why does the author put this information in sidebars and not in the main article?

   _____

   _____

   _____

   _____

   _____

3. How are the sidebars about weather folklore different from the other sidebars and the article?

_____

_____

_____

_____

_____

_____

4. Look at pages 8 and 9 in the magazine, the section of the article titled Map Time. What does this section explain?

_____

_____

_____

_____

5. Look more closely at the map on pages 8 and 9. What can a meteorologist tell about the weather on either side of the cold front?

_____

_____

_____

_____

6. How does the section titled Map Time support the main idea of this article?

_____

_____

_____

_____

_____

7. How do the pictures and captions on pages 5 and 6 help you understand the text? What other graphics could the author have included?

_____

_____

_____

_____

_____

8. What are four reasons authors write nonfiction?

_____

_____

9. The author's main purpose for writing "Forecasting the Weather" is to inform. Reread the last page of the article. What other purpose might the author have for writing? Why do you think this?

_____

_____

_____

_____

_____

_____

_____

_____

_____

10. Do you think the author does a good job in this article of explaining how weather forecasting works? Why or why not?

_____

_____

_____

_____

Explore "Let It Rain"

Sequence Events in the Text: The Water Cycle

Fill in the steps of the water cycle in sequence. Use the diagram on page 17 of the magazine to help you. Look in the text on page 16 for order words such as *first*, *next*, and *once*.

Steps in the Water Cycle

First

Next

Then

Finally

Write a summary of the water cycle in your own words. Keep the sequence of events in order. Use order words such as *first, second, next, then, finally,* and *at last*.

_____

_____

_____

_____

_____

_____

_____

_____

_____

_____

_____

_____

Explore "Let It Rain"

Sequence Events in the Text: Acid Rain Formation

Fill in the steps that produce acid rain. Use the sidebar on page 19 of the magazine to help you. Use order words in your chart, such as *first*, *next*, *then*, and *finally*.

> **Steps in Acid Rain Formation**

> **First**

↓

> **Next**

↓

> **Then**

↓

> **Finally**

Write a summary of how acid rain forms in your own words. Keep the sequence of events in order. Use order words such as *first, second, next, then, finally,* and *at last.*

_____

_____

_____

_____

_____

_____

_____

_____

_____

_____

_____

_____

_____

Explore "Winter Storms"
Compare and Contrast Nonfiction Texts

Compare and contrast the website booklet "Winter Storms" with the
magazine article "Winter Storms."

Similar	Different

LITERATURE & COMPREHENSION

Answer the questions in complete sentences.

1. Which text has more facts about what winter weather is? Support your answer with examples from the text.

   _____

   _____

   _____

   _____

2. Which text has more information about what to do in winter weather? Support your answer with examples from the text.

   _____

   _____

   _____

   _____

3. Which text has better graphics—diagrams, maps, pictures, and charts? Give reasons for your opinion.

   _____

   _____

   _____

   _____

   _____

4. What do you think the magazine article "Winter Storms" could have done better?

_____

_____

_____

5. What do you think the website booklet "Winter Storms" could have done better?

_____

_____

_____

6. What do you think is the author's purpose in the magazine article "Winter Storms"?

_____

_____

_____

7. What do you think is the author's purpose in the website booklet "Winter Storms"?

_____

_____

_____

Explore "Wind"

Create Your Own Graphic

Using the following checklist, create a graphic that shows information from the magazine article "Wind."

☐ Choose information from the magazine article that you could put into a graphic. Ideas include the following:

- Different types of wind and their characteristics
- Tools to measure wind and what they do
- How a tornado or hurricane forms
- How windmills or wind turbines work
- Locations on a map of where famous storms occurred or where named winds come from
- Measurements of wind speeds at one location over time

☐ Use references such as an encyclopedia or the Internet to gather more facts about your topic. Your information should

- Tell three or more main events in sequence.
- Use signal words such as *first*, *next*, *then*, and *finally*.

☐ Think about which kind of graphic would best show your information. Choose one of the following types:

- map
- diagram
- chart
- graph

☐ Draw your graphic.

LANGUAGE ARTS PURPLE

Answer the following questions in complete sentences.

1. Why did you choose the type of graphic that you did?

   _____

   _____

   _____

2. How do you think your graphic will help a reader understand the information in it?

   _____

   _____

   _____

3. What other information could you add to your graphic to make it better?

   _____

   _____

   _____

4. What other graphics do you think the author could have used in "Wind"? Why?

   _____

   _____

   _____

Explore "Storm Chasers"
Compare and Contrast Nonfiction Texts

Complete the diagram to compare and contrast the website booklet "Tornadoes" and the magazine article "Storm Chasers."

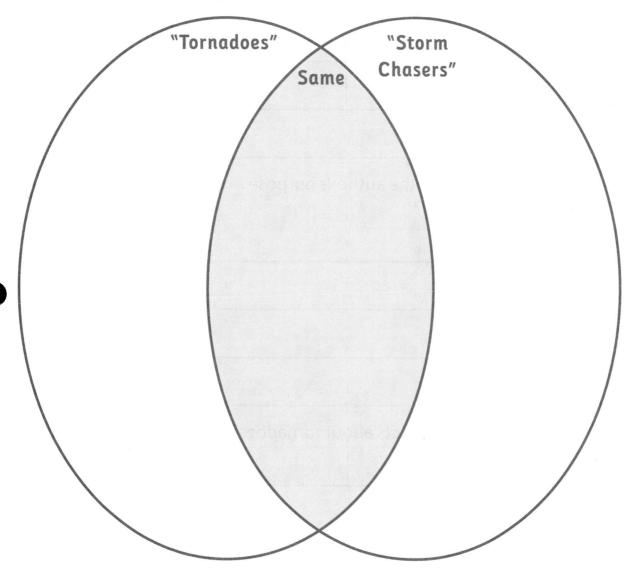

Answer the questions in complete sentences.

1. What do you think is the author's purpose in the magazine article "Storm Chasers"? Remember, the author may have more than one purpose.

_____

_____

_____

_____

2. What do you think is the author's purpose in the website booklet "Tornadoes"?

_____

_____

_____

_____

3. Which text has more facts about tornadoes? Why do you think this?

_____

_____

_____

_____

_____

4. Which text would you use if you wanted to know what to do in a tornado? Why?

_____

_____

_____

5. Which text has better graphics—diagrams, maps, pictures, and charts? Explain your answer.

_____

_____

_____

6. What did you like best about "Storm Chasers"? What did you like the least?

_____

_____

_____

7. What did you like best about "Tornadoes"? What did you like the least?

_____

_____

_____

_____

Reflections on *Weather or Not*
Make a Weather Cartoon

Follow the steps to make your own cartoon about a weather topic.

1. Pick a weather topic from the magazine *K¹² World: Weather or Not*.

2. Choose what you want to say about your topic. What is your main idea?

3. Gather at least four facts that support your main idea. You may use facts that you find in
   - The magazine *K¹² World: Weather or Not*
   - Library books, such as a nonfiction book about the weather or an article in an encyclopedia
   - A website with information about weather

4. Think of a fictional story related to your topic and imagine the characters.

5. Think of how you will tell the story. You may want to tell events in sequence or show cause and effect of a weather event.

6. Remember that you have two purposes: to inform and to entertain. Make the plot interesting, but also include facts.

7. Use the graphic organizer to plan your cartoon.

Answer the questions in complete sentences.

1. What is your weather topic?

   _____

2. What is the main idea of your cartoon about your topic?

   _____

   _____

3. List four details that support your main idea.

_____

_____

_____

_____

4. Who are your characters? Name and describe them.

_____

_____

_____

_____

5. What is the plot of your cartoon? List your events in sequence or use cause and effect to organize what happens.

_____

_____

_____

_____

_____

Make your cartoon in the boxes below, using all six spaces. Remember to include facts in your dialogue.

1	**2**
3	**4**
5	**6**

LITERATURE & COMPREHENSION

Explore Poems About Cats and Dogs

Evaluate Poems About Cats and Dogs

**Reread "The Hairy Dog," "I've Got a Dog," "A Kitten,"
and "Cat." Answer the questions in complete sentences.**

1. How does the language in the poems help you create a mental picture of the pets? Give examples from at least two poems.

   _____

   _____

   _____

   _____

   _____

   _____

2. Which poem best describes its pet? Why do you think this?

   _____

   _____

   _____

   _____

   _____

   _____

3. Which poem did you enjoy reading the most? Why?

_____

_____

_____

_____

_____

4. Choose one of the poems. How do you think the poet wants you to
feel about the pet in the poem? Do you feel this way?

_____

_____

_____

_____

_____

Explore "The Elephant" and "The Silent Snake"

Evaluate "The Elephant" and "The Silent Snake"

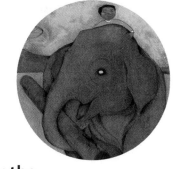

Reread "The Elephant" and "The Silent Snake." Answer the questions in complete sentences.

1. How do the similes in the poem "The Elephant" help you imagine what the elephant is like?

   _____

   _____

   _____

   _____

   _____

2. How do the vivid verbs in "The Silent Snake" help you imagine how the snake moves and sounds?

   _____

   _____

   _____

   _____

   _____

3. Which poem is better at describing its animal, "The Elephant" or "The Silent Snake"? Why do you think this?

_____

_____

_____

_____

4. Using at least one vivid verb, write a sentence to describe an elephant.

_____

_____

_____

5. Write a simile to describe a snake. Remember to use either *like* or *as* in your simile. Compare the snake to something else that will help your reader imagine the snake.

_____

_____

_____

_____

_____

_____

Reflections on Animal Friends Poetry
Write Your Own Animal Poem

Write a poem about an animal. Use your favorite poem in this unit as a model. Follow this checklist as you write, checking off each item as you go.

☐ Give your poem a title.

☐ Write at least two stanzas.

☐ Use a rhyme scheme for each stanza that follows this pattern: ABAB.

☐ Use at least one example of alliteration or onomatopoeia.

☐ Use sensory language.

☐ Use vivid verbs.

☐ Draw an illustration for your poem.

Write your poem here.

Title: _____

_____

_____

_____

_____

_____

_____

_____

_____

_____

_____

_____

_____

Illustrate your poem here.

When you have finished your poem, give a reading of your poem to an audience. Express yourself clearly and with emotion. Explain how your illustration connects to the poem and shows an image you tried to create with your words.

Explore *George Washington: Soldier, Hero, President* (A)

Create a Time Line

Tear out the two pages of the time line and tape them together to form one line. Then use your book to identify important dates and events from George Washington's life. Add them to the time line.

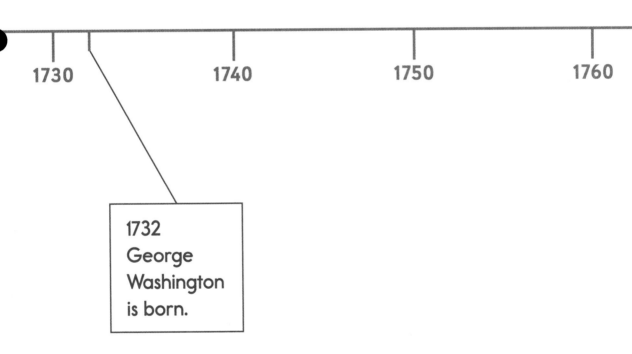

1730   1740   1750   1760

1732
George
Washington
is born.

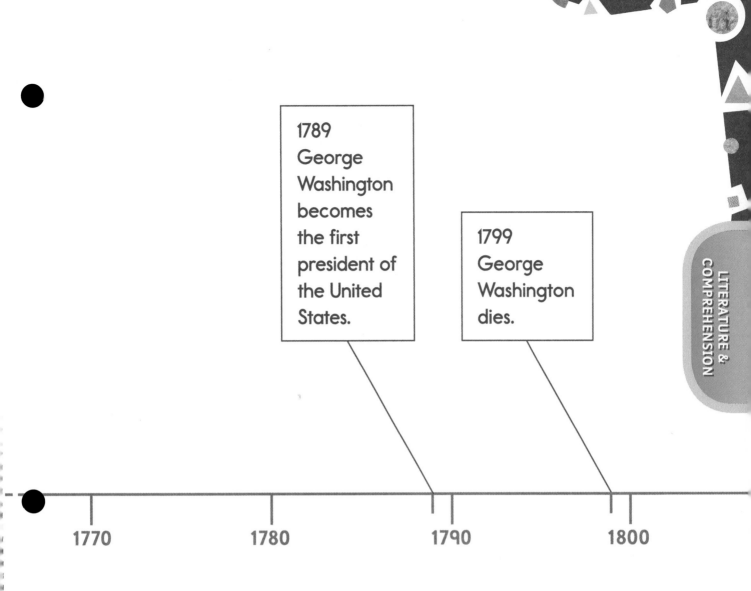

1789
George Washington becomes the first president of the United States.

1799
George Washington dies.

1770   1780   1790   1800

Explore *George Washington: Soldier, Hero, President* (C)

Identify George Washington's Traits

Write "George Washington" in the middle circle. Write one of George Washington's traits in each of the outer circles. Then give evidence from the book that shows this trait.

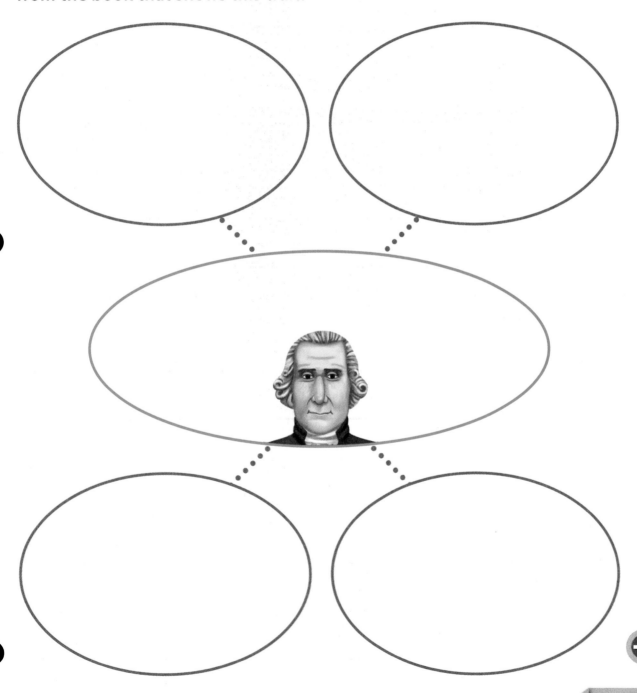

LITERATURE & COMPREHENSION

Use your web on George Washington's traits to answer the following questions in complete sentences.

1. The main idea of a piece of writing is the most important point the author makes. What is the main idea of the book *George Washington: Soldier, Hero, President*?

_____

_____

_____

_____

_____

_____

2. What is the authors' purpose in writing this book? Give reasons to support your idea.

_____

_____

_____

_____

_____

_____

LITERATURE & COMPREHENSION

Reflections on *George Washington: Soldier, Hero, President*

Write an Article About George Washington

Imagine you are a reporter planning to write a newspaper article about the life of George Washington.

- Think about the main idea of *George Washington: Soldier, Hero, President*. Then decide what the main idea of your article will be.
- Choose events from your time line about Washington's life to include in your article.
- Review your trait web and decide how you will describe George Washington.
- Decide what your purpose for writing the article is: to inform, to entertain, to persuade, or to give an opinion.
- Follow the steps to write a first draft of your article.

1. Headline (catchy way to state the topic of your article):

    _____

    _____

    _____

2. by (your name): _____

LITERATURE & COMPREHENSION

3. Introduction: Write your first paragraph. Answer these questions:
   - Who is the article about?
   - What did he do that was important?
   - Where did he live?
   - When did he live?
   - Why should we remember him?
   - How did he act as a person?

   _____

   _____

   _____

   _____

   _____

4. Body: Write one or two paragraphs for the middle. Make sure you
   - Summarize at least three main events in Washington's life.
   - Include the dates of the events and tell them in sequence.
   - Describe the traits that Washington showed with his actions.

   _____

   _____

   _____

   _____

   _____

_____

_____

_____

_____

_____

_____

5. Conclusion: Write the last paragraph of your article. Make sure you
   - Summarize the main idea of your article.
   - Tell why Washington should be remembered.

_____

_____

_____

_____

_____

_____

Semester Review
Practice Responding in Writing

Read the two stories, and then answer the questions.

The Jay and the Peacocks

adapted from Aesop's fables

Once there was a jay who wanted to be a peacock. "Peacocks are such fine, beautiful birds," he thought. "They have such bright, colorful feathers that shine blue and green in the sun. And look at me just a plain, brown bird. Oh, I wish I could be a peacock!"

One morning, the jay flew down into the yard where the peacocks liked to walk. Peacock feathers were lying around the yard, glowing like blue-green jewels in the sun. The jay collected all the cast-off peacock feathers, tied them to his tail, and walked down to the peacocks. "How fine I look!" he thought.

But when the jay got close to the peacocks, they saw that he was only pretending. So they pecked at him and tore away all his fake feathers.

The jay was embarrassed. He flew back to sit with the other jays.

But the other jays had watched him from the trees. They were angry with him, too. As they flew away, they cried, "Fine feathers do not make fine birds."

The Peacock and the Crane

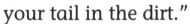

adapted from Aesop's fables

A peacock passed by a crane. The peacock spread its beautiful tail. It made fun of the crane's dull gray feathers.

"Look at me! I am dressed like a king, in all the bright colors of the rainbow," the peacock boasted. "You, however, have no color on your wings."

"This is true," answered the crane. "But I can fly as high as the heavens. My voice rises to the stars when I sing. You, on the other hand, can hardly fly at all. You are left to walk on the ground and drag your tail in the dirt."

As the peacock marched off, the crane said, "Fine feathers do not make fine birds."

1. What kind of stories are these?

   _____

2. Summarize "The Jay and the Peacocks."

   _____

   _____

   _____

3. What does the jay do in "The Jay and the Peacocks"?

   _____

   _____

4. How do the jay's actions affect the peacocks?

   _____

   _____

5. How do the jay's actions affect the other jays?

   _____

   _____

6. What sentence from "The Jay and the Peacocks" tells the moral?

   _____

   _____

7. Write the moral of "The Jay and the Peacocks" in your own words.

_____

_____

_____

_____

_____

8. Summarize "The Peacock and the Crane."

_____

_____

_____

9. What does the peacock do in "The Peacock and the Crane"?

_____

_____

10. How do the peacock's actions affect the crane?

_____

_____

11. What sentence from "The Peacock and the Crane" tells the moral?

_____

_____

12. Write the moral of "The Peacock and the Crane" in your own words.

_____

_____

_____

_____

13. Write a paragraph in which you compare and contrast the two fables.

_____

_____

_____

_____

_____

_____

_____

_____

_____

Writing Skills

Kinds of Sentences
Write Different Kinds of Sentences

Follow the directions to write each kind of sentence.

1. Write an **interrogative sentence** about the moon.

   _____

   _____

   _____

2. Write an **imperative sentence** about manners at the dinner table.

   _____

   _____

   _____

3. Write a **declarative sentence** about winter.

   _____

   _____

   _____

4. Write an **exclamatory sentence** about your best friend.

   _____

   _____

   _____

Simple Sentences (A)

Write Simple Sentences

Write three sentences. Use the subjects and predicates in the word bank in your sentences.

Subject	Predicate
Jim	was a lot of fun.
The swim lesson	has many tall trees.
The park	ran for a touchdown.

1. _____

   _____

2. _____

   _____

3. _____

   _____

Write a simple sentence of your own. Make yourself the subject, and tell about something that you like to do.

4. _____

   _____

Simple Sentences (B)

Write Simple Sentences with Compound Parts

Write a compound subject for each simple sentence.

1. _____

   _____ went to the beach.

2. _____

   _____ rumbled by.

Write a compound predicate for each simple sentence.

3. The door _____

   _____

4. A grandmother _____

   _____

Write a simple sentence with a compound subject about eating pancakes.

5. _____

   _____

Write a simple sentence with a compound predicate about a cat.

6. _____

   _____

WRITING SKILLS

Compound Sentences (A)
Simple or Compound?

Write _S_ if the sentence is a simple sentence. Write _C_ if the sentence is a compound sentence.

WRITING SKILLS

1. Tie your shoes, or you will trip. _____

2. The sand is white and soft. _____

3. Clowns and jugglers perform at the circus. _____

4. Mr. Lu was friendly, yet he sometimes lost his temper. _____

5. I solved the math problem and wrote the answer. _____

6. Norr Street runs one way, and Vine Street runs the other. _____

Underline the conjunction in the compound sentence.

7. The fish was blue, so we could not see it in the water.

8. I'm not tired, yet it is bedtime.

Add a conjunction to the sentence.

9. Wildwood has a boardwalk, _____ Sea Isle has nice shops.

Compound Sentences (B)
Use Commas in Compound Sentences

Place a comma in the compound sentence.

1. Everyone else is happy so I'm happy, too.

2. Columbus sailed for months yet he did not reach India.

3. Thanks for the card but my birthday was last month.

4. You have pen on your shirt and chalk is on your pants.

Make the two simple sentences into a compound sentence using the conjunction *and*.

5. Gretchen told a joke.
   Pam laughed.

   _____

   _____

Make the two simple sentences into a compound sentence using the conjunction *so*.

6. Joel was chilly.
   Alex gave him a hat.

   _____

   _____

WRITING SKILLS

Complex Sentences (A)

Use Complex Sentences

Choose sentence parts from the word bank to write complex sentences. Use one dependent part and one independent part for each sentence. Add a comma if needed.

Dependent parts	Independent parts
because you asked	I dropped all the strawberries
before we came home	we picked out some fruit
as I was carrying the fruit to the car	I'll tell you the story
while we were shopping	we stopped at the farm stand

1. _____

    _____

2. _____

    _____

3. _____

    _____

4. _____

    _____

WRITING SKILLS

Complex Sentences (B)
Use Conjunctions in Complex Sentences

Circle the conjunction that makes the sentence a complex sentence.

1. (Since,   So) Mark lived there, he knew the directions.

2. Jo missed the game (because,   or) she overslept.

Complete the complex sentence by filling in the blank with an independent part.

3. _____ before the show began.

Complete the complex sentence by filling in the blank with a dependent part.

4. _____, take the cake out of the oven.

Write a complex sentence that uses the conjunction *if* and begins with a dependent part.

5. _____

_____

Model Opinion Paragraph
Model Opinion Paragraph

Use Alexander's opinion paragraph as you work through the lessons in this unit.

Kickball

If you want to have a good time, play kickball. Kickball is fun because lots of people can play at once. Since you have to run a lot, you get great exercise. Kickball is easy to play, too, because you only need a ball, a field, and some friends. There are lots of ways to spend a sunny day, but kickball is the best way.

topic sentence

transition

supporting reasons

concluding sentence

Model Opinion Paragraph

Respond to the Model Opinion Paragraph

Answer the questions about Alexander's opinion paragraph.

1. How does Alexander feel about kickball?

    _____

    _____

2. Where does Alexander tell his opinion about kickball?

    _____

    _____

3. What three reasons does Alexander give for having this opinion?

    _____

    _____

    _____

4. Why are transitions like *because* and *since* important in Alexander's paragraph?

    _____

    _____

5. Where does Alexander restate his opinion about kickball?

    _____

    _____

6. Alexander does not include reasons or facts in his paragraph that are unrelated to his opinion about kickball. Why not?

_____

_____

_____

_____

_____

Brainstorm Topics
Brainstorm and Choose Your Topic

First, read the assignment for writing your opinion paragraph. Then, write as many possible ideas for your paragraph as you can think of. After that, cross off ideas until you have one left. That idea is your topic. Circle it.

Write a paragraph that expresses your opinion on a topic.

- Focus on one main idea. The main idea should state your opinion on the topic and should be your first sentence. This sentence is also called the topic sentence.
- Include at least two reasons that support your opinion.
- Write at least four sentences for your paragraph.
- End with a concluding sentence.
- Be sure a reader can understand your opinion and your reasons for it.

Plan Your Paragraph
Gather and Organize Your Ideas

Complete the graphic organizer to plan your opinion paragraph.

> ### Main Idea

↓

> ### Supporting Reason

⋮

> ### Supporting Reason

⋮

> ### Supporting Reason

↓

> ### Conclusion

Draft Your Opinion Paragraph (A)
Write Your Draft

Read the assignment. Use your Gather and Organize Your Ideas page to help you write the first draft of your opinion paragraph. Write only on the white rows. You will use the purple rows for revisions later.

Write a paragraph that expresses your opinion on a topic.

- Focus on one main idea. The main idea should state your opinion on the topic and should be your first sentence. This sentence is also called the topic sentence.

- Include at least two reasons that support your opinion.

- Write at least four sentences for your paragraph.

- End with a concluding sentence.

- Be sure a reader can understand your opinion and your reasons for it.

Start here ▶

LANGUAGE ARTS PURPLE

Draft Your Opinion Paragraph (B)
Tell Me About My Paragraph

Have another person read your opinion paragraph and answer the questions.

1. What is the topic, or main idea, of the paragraph, and what is the writer's opinion about it?

   _____

   _____

   _____

2. What reasons does the writer give for having this opinion?

   _____

   _____

   _____

3. Does the writer use transition words to connect ideas and help the paragraph read smoothly? If not, where are transitions needed?

   _____

   _____

   _____

4. Does the writer restate the opinion in a conclusion?

   _____

   _____

5. Are any sentences unrelated to the topic? If so, which ones?

_____

_____

6. What else would you like to know about the writer's opinion?

_____

_____

_____

_____

_____

_____

Use a Dictionary and Thesaurus
Use the Tools

Use a dictionary to find the meaning of the underlined word. Write that word's definition in the space. The dictionary you use may be a printed book or online.

1. The house had huge <u>pillars</u> in front of it.

    Definition: _____

    _____

2. No one told me I'd get in trouble for being <u>tardy</u>.

    Definition: _____

3. Most of the desserts are <u>tortes</u>.

    Definition: _____

    _____

Use a thesaurus to find a synonym or antonym of the underlined word. Write one of the synonyms or antonyms you find in the space. The thesaurus you use may be a printed book or online.

4. I was <u>surprised</u> to see that you cut your hair.

    Synonym: _____

5. The hummingbird's wings flap very <u>slowly</u>.

    Antonym: _____

6. The waiter was quite <u>gracious</u>, and he forgot to bring my soup, too.

    Antonym: _____

Revise Your Paragraph
Revise with a Checklist

Follow this checklist as you revise the draft of your opinion paragraph. Check off each box after you complete each item.

- ☐ Check that the paragraph tells about one topic.

- ☐ Check that the paragraph expresses an opinion about the topic.

- ☐ Check that the topic sentence clearly states your opinion.

- ☐ Add transitions to connect opinions and reasons.

- ☐ Remove reasons that are unimportant, unnecessary, or do not support your opinion.

- ☐ Simplify or shorten sentences that are too long.

- ☐ Use a thesaurus to improve word choice.

WRITING SKILLS

Proofread Your Paragraph
Proofread with a Checklist

Follow this checklist as you proofread the draft of your opinion paragraph. Check off each box after you complete each item.

- ☐ Check that all sentences begin with a capital letter.

- ☐ Check that all sentences end with the correct punctuation mark.

- ☐ Fix sentence fragments. You may need to add a subject or predicate.

- ☐ Check spellings of any words you don't know by looking them up in the dictionary.

- ☐ Check that you have not made any errors by using homophones of words.

WRITING SKILLS

Publish Your Paragraph

Publish Your Opinion Paragraph

Write the final copy of your opinion paragraph in your best handwriting. Write a title for your paragraph on the first line.

_____

_____

_____

_____

_____

_____

_____

_____

_____

_____

_____

_____

WRITING SKILLS

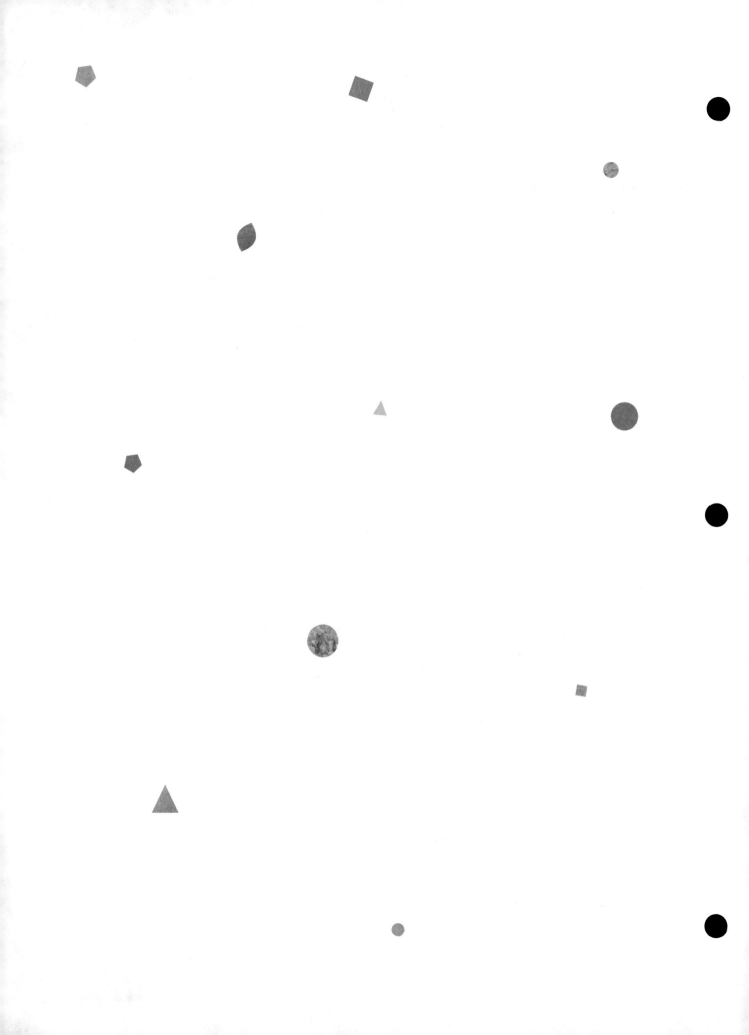

Complete Predicates and Model Personal Story

Model Personal Story

Use Winnie's personal story as you work through the lessons in this unit.

The Big Drop

by Winnie

hook → Click, click, click. On the ride to the top, the roller coaster clicked. Thump, thump, thump. My heart beat really fast. Next to me was my friend, Marc. In front of us were a few feet of track. Below us were all the people at Astroland. I gripped Marc's hand, and the wind blew my hair. We were at the top of the hill.

— beginning of story

Whoosh! Down we went. The ground came closer. The people seemed to be getting bigger. I screamed, and I think I heard Marc scream, too. There was lots of shaking and rumbling. Then we zoomed up. That's when I started to have fun. I smiled and shouted with joy. We laughed the whole time.

— middle of story

importance of event →

Screech! The roller coaster came to a stop.
Marc and I were the first ones out. We ran
so fast that it felt like we were flying. We ran
to our families. Mom took our picture, and
Marc's uncle Jerry gave us high fives. My dad
said he was proud of us for riding a roller
coaster all by ourselves for the first time. I was
proud of myself, too, because I had faced one
of my biggest fears. But I only had one thing
to say—I wanted to know when I could ride
it again!

end of story

....

Complete Predicates and Model Personal Story

Respond to the Model Personal Story

Answer the questions about Winnie's personal story.

1. What is Winnie's personal story about?

   _____

   _____

   _____

   _____

2. How does Winnie capture the attention of readers in her first paragraph?

   _____

   _____

   _____

   _____

   _____

   _____

   _____

WRITING SKILLS

3. Winnie's story is in chronological order. Imagine that she wanted to add a new detail about what happened *before* she and Marc got on the roller coaster. Which paragraph would she add it to? Why?

_____

_____

_____

_____

_____

4. Why is this experience important enough for Winnie to write about?

_____

_____

_____

5. How did Winnie feel once the roller coaster ride was over? How do you know?

_____

_____

_____

_____

Combine Sentences and Brainstorm Your Topic

Brainstorm and Choose Your Topic

First, read the assignment for writing your personal story. Then, write as many possible topics for your personal story as you can think of. After that, cross off ideas until you have one left. That idea is your topic. Circle it.

> Tell a true story about a meaningful experience in your life.
>
> - Describe the experience from start to finish.
> - Use chronological order.
> - Include important details about what happened, who else was there, and how you felt at the time.
> - Be sure a reader can tell why this experience is important to you.

Combine Sentences and Plan Your Personal Story

Gather and Organize Your Ideas

Fill in the form with details about your personal story.

My story topic _____

_____

Who? _____

_____

What? _____

_____

When? _____

_____

Where? _____

_____

Complete the graphic organizer to plan your personal story.

Topic _____

```
┌─────────────────────────────────────────────────────┐
│                     Beginning                         │
│                                                       │
│                                                       │
│                                                       │
│                                                       │
└─────────────────────────────────────────────────────┘
                           │
                           ▼
┌─────────────────────────────────────────────────────┐
│                      Middle                           │
│                                                       │
│                                                       │
│                                                       │
│                                                       │
│                                                       │
└─────────────────────────────────────────────────────┘
                           │
                           ▼
┌─────────────────────────────────────────────────────┐
│                       End                             │
│                                                       │
│                                                       │
│                                                       │
│                                                       │
└─────────────────────────────────────────────────────┘
```

Importance to me _____

Draft Your Personal Story
Write Your Draft

Read the assignment. Use your Gather and Organize Your Ideas page to help you write the first draft of your personal story. Write only on the white rows. You will use the purple rows for revisions later.

Tell a true story about a meaningful experience in your life.

- Describe the experience from start to finish.
- Use chronological order.
- Include important details about what happened, who else was there, and how you felt at the time.
- Be sure a reader can tell why this experience was important to you.

Start here ▶

LANGUAGE ARTS PURPLE

Combine Sentences and Draft Your Personal Story

Tell Me About My Story

Have another person read your personal story and answer the questions.

1. What is the story about?

    _____

2. Who are the characters?

    _____

3. What is the setting?

    _____

4. What happens in the beginning, middle, and end of the story?

    _____

    _____

    _____

5. What kind of order is used in the story?

    _____

6. Is there anything else you would like to know about the story?

    _____

    _____

    _____

WRITING SKILLS

7. Are there details that could have been left out of the story?

_____

_____

_____

_____

8. Why is the story important to the writer?

_____

_____

_____

9. What did you like best about the story?

_____

_____

_____

Improve Sentences with Details
Add Details to Sentences

Read the basic sentence. Think about some details you can add to make it come to life. Write two of those details in the spaces given. The first one has been done for you.

1. **The birds sing.**

   Detail about how the birds look <u>large and colorful</u>

   Detail about how they sing <u>loudly</u>

2. **Five boys run.**

   Detail about what the boys wear _____

   Detail about where they run _____

3. **The wind blows.**

   Detail about how the wind feels _____

   Detail about what the wind blows _____

4. **A bus passes.**

   Detail about how the bus sounds _____

   Detail about what the bus passes _____

5. **Two dogs bark.**

   Detail about how the dogs look _____

   Detail about what the dogs bark at _____

WRITING SKILLS

Add at least two details to each sentence. Write your new and improved sentence. The first one has been done for you.

6. Amy slips.

   My sister Amy slips on the wet floor.

7. My uncle laughs.

   _____

8. The lion roars.

   _____

9. Jake points.

   _____

10. Three snakes slither.

    _____

11. The pizza bakes.

    _____

12. The ice cream melts.

    _____

Revise Your Personal Story
Revise with a Checklist

Follow this checklist as you revise the draft of your personal story. Check off each box after you complete each item.

☐ Check that the story tells about one main experience.

☐ Remove details that are unimportant or unnecessary.

☐ Check that the story has a clear beginning, middle, and end.

☐ Check that events are told in chronological order.

☐ Combine sentences that have similar parts.

☐ Add details to expand short sentences.

☐ Include a statement about why this experience was meaningful, if it is not obvious.

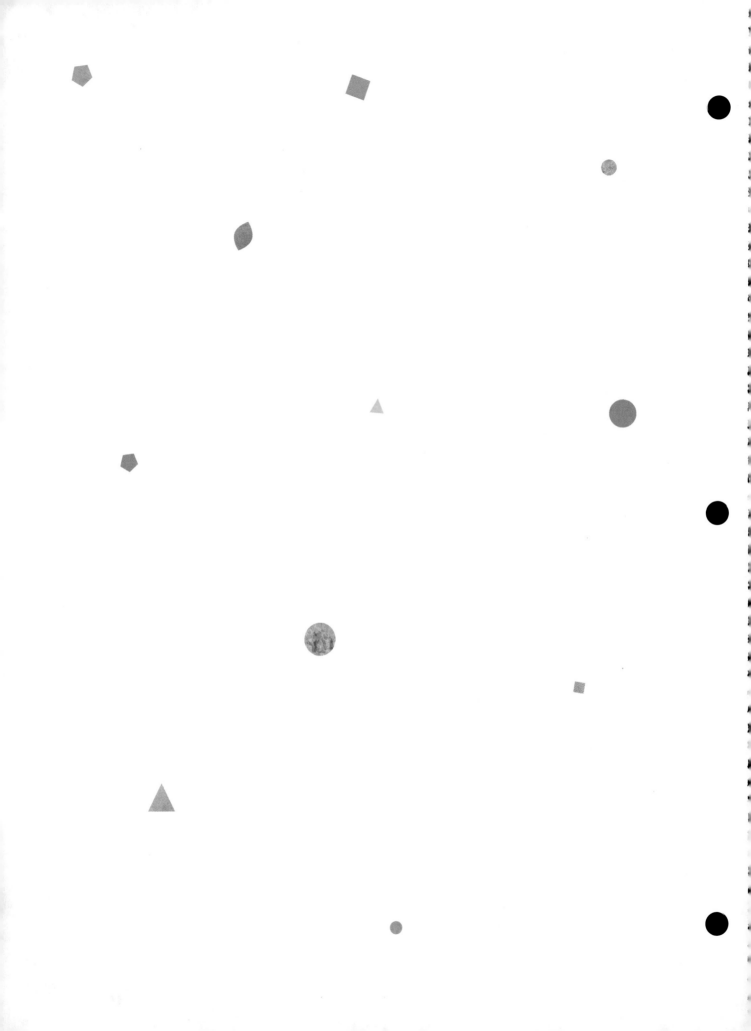

Unit Review and Proofread Your Personal Story

Proofread with a Checklist

Follow this checklist as you proofread the draft of your personal story. Check off each box after you complete each item.

☐ Check that all sentences begin with a capital letter.

☐ Check that all sentences end with the correct punctuation mark.

☐ Fix sentence fragments. You may need to add a subject or predicate.

☐ Add a comma before a conjunction in a compound sentence.

☐ Check the spelling of any words you don't know by looking them up in the dictionary.

Unit Checkpoint and Publish Your Personal Story

Publish Your Personal Story

Write the final copy of your personal story in your best handwriting. Write a title for your story on the first line.

_____

_____

_____

_____

_____

_____

_____

_____

_____

_____

_____

_____

_____

_____

_____

_____

_____

_____

_____

_____

_____

_____

LANGUAGE ARTS PURPLE

Model Personal Letter
Model Friendly Letter

Use Ron's letter as you work through the lessons in the unit.

heading →

9 Biddle Way
Los Angeles, CA 90056
March 17, 2012

greeting → Dear Jen,

body →

I got your last letter on Monday. Thanks for sending the picture of you playing your guitar. It made me miss you a lot, but I have some great news. We're getting a piano!

Mom and Dad told me yesterday. I was so excited that I jumped all around the room. They said that our neighbors are moving, and they don't have a place for their piano in the new house. So they are giving it to us.

I'm not sure where the piano is going to go. I would like to have it in my room. Mom wants to put it in the basement. Dad said he thinks we should keep it in the living room. I guess we'll have to wait and see.

The best part is that we want you to visit this summer and bring your guitar. Mom and Dad said you can stay for as long as you want! Isn't that great? We can play songs together every day and even have a concert! So write me back if you want to come. I'll be waiting!

closing → Your friend,

signature → Ron

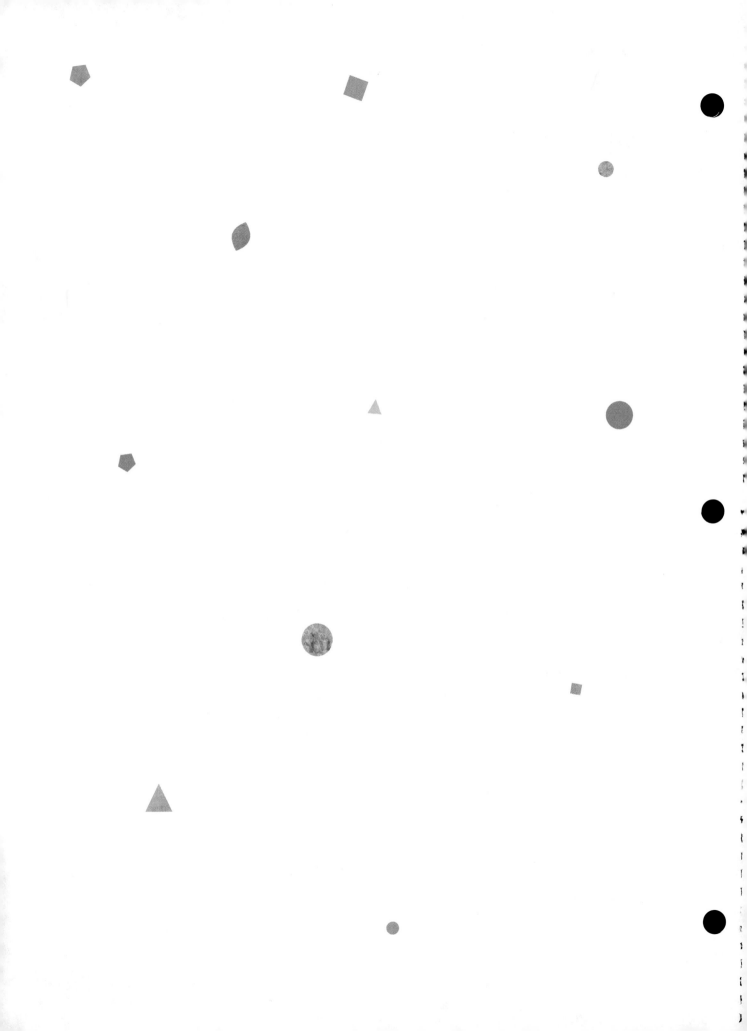

Model Personal Letter

Respond to the Model Friendly Letter

Answer the questions about Ron's personal letter.

1. What information does Ron include in the heading of his letter?

    _____

2. What closing does Ron use in this letter?

    _____

3. Write one other greeting Ron might have used in this letter.

    _____

4. Who is the audience for Ron's letter?

    _____

5. Why did Ron write this letter?

    _____

    _____

    _____

6. Describe the voice and tone of Ron's letter.

    _____

    _____

    _____

    _____

WRITING SKILLS

7. Why does Ron use four paragraphs in his letter?

_____

_____

_____

_____

_____

_____

_____

Heading of a Letter and Plan a Friendly Letter

Brainstorm Friendly Letter Topics and Organize Your Ideas

First, read the assignment for writing your personal letter. Then, write at least five ideas for a friendly letter. Think about what news, thoughts, or feelings you want to share. Also think about whom you want to share with. When you have finished, circle the idea you want to use for the topic of your friendly letter.

Write a personal letter.

- Choose your purpose.
- Identify your audience.
- Write the information, thoughts, and ideas you want to share.
- Begin a new paragraph for each new idea.
- Remember to include a heading, greeting, body, closing, and signature.

_____   _____

_____   _____

_____   _____

_____   _____

_____   _____

Answer the questions about the kind of letter you are planning.

What kind of letter are you planning?

☐ Friendly Letter   ☐ Thank-You Letter   ☐ Invitation

What is your purpose? _____

_____

_____

Who is your audience? _____

_____

What information will you include in the body of your letter? _____

_____

_____

_____

_____

_____

_____

WRITING SKILLS

Greeting & Closing of a Letter and Plan a Thank-You Letter

Brainstorm Thank-You Letter Topics and Organize Your Ideas

First, read the assignment for writing your personal letter. Then, write at least five ideas for a thank-you letter. Think about what you have to be thankful for and the people who may have helped you or given you things. When you have finished, circle the topic you want to use for your thank-you letter.

Write a personal letter.

- Choose your purpose.
- Identify your audience.
- Write the information, thoughts, and ideas you want to share.
- Begin a new paragraph for each new idea.
- Remember to include a heading, greeting, body, closing, and signature.

_____   _____

_____   _____

_____   _____

_____   _____

_____   _____

_____   _____

Answer the questions about the kind of letter you are planning.

What kind of letter are you planning?

☐ Friendly Letter   ☐ Thank-You Letter   ☐ Invitation

What is your purpose? _____

_____

_____

Who is your audience? _____

_____

What information will you include in the body of your letter? _____

_____

_____

_____

_____

_____

_____

_____

Addresses and Plan a Letter of Invitation

Brainstorm Invitation Topics and Organize Your Ideas

First, read the assignment for writing your personal letter. Then, write at least five ideas for a letter of invitation. Think about upcoming events and celebrations and whom you'd like to share them with. When you have finished, circle the topic you want to use for your letter of invitation.

> Write a personal letter.
>
> - Choose your purpose.
> - Identify your audience.
> - Write the information, thoughts, and ideas you want to share.
> - Begin a new paragraph for each new idea.
> - Remember to include a heading, greeting, body, closing, and signature.

_____   _____

_____   _____

_____   _____

_____   _____

_____   _____

_____   _____

Answer the questions about the kind of letter you are planning.

What kind of letter are you planning?

☐ Friendly Letter   ☐ Thank-You Letter   ☐ Invitation

What is your purpose? _____

_____

_____

Who is your audience? _____

_____

What information will you include in the body of your letter? _____

_____

_____

_____

_____

_____

_____

_____

_____

Draft Your Personal Letter
Write Your Draft

Read the assignment. Use your personal letter planning form to help you write the first draft of your personal letter. Write only on the white rows. You will use the purple rows for revisions later.

> Write a personal letter.
> - Choose your purpose.
> - Identify your audience.
> - Write the information, thoughts, and ideas you want to share.
> - Begin a new paragraph for each new idea.
> - Remember to include a heading, greeting, body, closing, and signature.

Start here ▶

LANGUAGE ARTS PURPLE

Draft Your Personal Letter
Tell Me About My Letter

Have another person read your letter and answer the questions.

1. What is the topic and purpose of the letter?

   _____

   _____

2. Who is the writer's audience?

   _____

3. Does the letter have a heading, greeting, body, closing, and signature? If not, what is missing?

   _____

4. Where does the writer state the purpose of the letter?

   _____

5. Are any sentences unrelated to the topic or the purpose of the letter? If so, which ones?

   _____

   _____

   _____

   _____

   _____

WRITING SKILLS

6. What did you like best about the letter?

_____

_____

_____

_____

_____

_____

LANGUAGE ARTS PURPLE

Letters as E-mails
Write an E-mail

Choose two people to send an e-mail to. If you know their e-mail addresses, write them in the proper places. If you do not, it's okay to make them up. Write a word or two to describe your message in the subject field. Then, write a short e-mail that has a greeting, at least two body sentences, a closing, and a signature.

Send	To:	
	Cc:	
	Subject:	

Revise Your Personal Letter
Revise with a Checklist

Follow this checklist as you revise the draft of your personal letter. Check off each box after you complete each item.

☐ Check that the letter's purpose is clear.

☐ Check that the voice and tone fit the audience.

☐ Include all important ideas or details.

☐ Properly place all ideas and details in the letter.

☐ Remove ideas and details that are unimportant or unnecessary.

☐ Include a heading, greeting, body, closing, and signature.

☐ Combine sentences that are similar.

☐ Add details to expand short sentences.

☐ Shorten sentences that are too long.

☐ Use a thesaurus to improve word choice.

Unit Review and Proofread Your Personal Letter

Proofread with a Checklist

Follow this checklist as you proofread the draft of your letter. Check off each box after you complete each item.

- ☐ Use a comma between the city and state and the day and the year in the heading of the letter.

- ☐ Begin the greeting with a capital letter and end with a comma.

- ☐ Indent each body paragraph.

- ☐ Begin only the first word of the closing with a capital letter.

- ☐ End the closing with a comma.

- ☐ Begin the signature with a capital letter.

- ☐ Look up unknown words in the dictionary to check their spelling.

Unit Checkpoint and Publish Your Personal Letter

Publish Your Personal Letter

Write the final copy of your personal letter in your best handwriting. Remember to include a heading, greeting, body, closing, and signature.

_____

_____

_____

_____

_____

_____

_____

_____

_____

_____

_____

_____

_____

_____

_____

_____

_____

_____

_____

_____

_____

_____

_____

_____

Collective, Abstract, & Compound Nouns and Model Informative Essay

Model Informative Essay

Use Serena's informative essay as you work through the lessons in this unit.

title ⟶ **The Truth About Bats**

topic sentence ⟶ Bats may look scary, but you don't have to be afraid of them. I know

details ⟶ because I used to be scared of bats. I thought they were ugly and mean. I thought they hurt people. I even had bad dreams about bats. Then I went to the Lincoln County Zoo. That's where I learned what bats are really like.

— introduction

topic sentence ⟶ At the zoo, I learned that bats are really interesting animals. They cannot see well, but they have great

facts ⟶ hearing. They sleep during the day and are awake at night. Bats are much smaller than I thought, too. They look like mice with wings. I still think they are ugly, but they are not mean. They mostly eat insects, and they try to stay away from people. So if you don't bother a bat, it probably won't bother you.

— body

WRITING SKILLS

topic sentence → I am not afraid of bats anymore. I know that real bats are not like bats in stories or movies. Now my dreams about bats are not scary ones. They just make me want to learn more!

— conclusion

Collective, Abstract, & Compound Nouns and Model Informative Essay

Respond to the Model Informative Essay

Answer the questions about Serena's informative essay.

1. What is the topic of Serena's informative essay?

   _____

2. What is the first paragraph of Serena's informative essay called?

   _____

3. In which paragraph does Serena provide most of the information about her topic? What is this paragraph called?

   _____

4. What is the last paragraph of Serena's informative essay called?

   _____

5. What is the topic sentence of the second paragraph?

   _____

   _____

6. Describe one fact that Serena includes in the second paragraph.

   _____

   _____

WRITING SKILLS

7. What is one detail that Serena includes in the final paragraph?

_____

_____

8. Are you surprised by what Serena says in the final paragraph? Why or why not?

_____

_____

_____

9. What is one fact you learned from Serena's informative essay?

_____

_____

Singular & Plural Nouns and Brainstorm Topics

Brainstorm and Choose Your Topic

First, read the assignment for writing your informative essay.

> Write an informative essay.
>
> - Think about your purpose and audience.
> - Begin with an introduction that states your topic and tells why it is important.
> - Write information about your topic in the body of the essay. Be sure to use facts, definitions, and details.
> - End with a conclusion that wraps up the essay in an interesting way.
> - Include an illustration about your topic.

Next, begin planning your informative essay by brainstorming topics. Write as many topics as you can think of for your informative essay. To help you get started, ask yourself these questions:

- **What are some topics that I know a lot about?**
- **What are some topics that I want to tell others about?**

_____

_____

_____

_____

_____

_____

_____

_____

_____

_____

_____

_____

_____

_____

As you look over your list of topics, ask yourself the following questions about each one:

- **Is this topic really interesting to me?**
- **Will this topic be interesting to my readers?**
- **Do I know enough about this topic to write an essay about it?**
- **Is this topic too complicated?**
- **Is this topic too simple?**

Based on your answers, choose one topic and circle it. This is the topic for your essay.

Plan Your Informative Essay
Gather and Organize Your Ideas

Complete the graphic organizer to plan your informative essay.

Audience _____

Purpose _____

> **Introduction: My Topic and How I Know About It**

> **Body: Information About the Topic**

> **Conclusion: Why the Topic Is Important**

Draw a picture that illustrates an important part of your informative essay, such as a fact or idea. Write a short caption under your picture that describes or explains it.

LANGUAGE ARTS PURPLE

Plan Your Informative Essay
Tell Me About My Plan

Have another person read the graphic organizer for your informative essay and answer the questions.

1. Does the box for the introduction name the essay's topic and explain how the writer knows about it?

   A. Yes   **B.** No

2. How might the writer improve the ideas for the introduction?

   _____

3. Does the box for the body give useful information about the topic?

   A. Yes   **B.** No

4. How might the writer improve the ideas for the body?

   _____

5. Does the box for the conclusion explain why the topic is important?

   A. Yes   **B.** No

6. How might the writer improve the ideas for the conclusion?

   _____

7. Look at the picture the writer drew. Does it help make the ideas and points in the essay's plan clearer?

   A. Yes   **B.** No

Singular Possessive Nouns and Draft Your Informative Essay
Write Your Draft

Read the assignment. Use your graphic organizer to help you write the first draft of your informative essay. Write only on the white rows. You will use the purple rows for revisions later.

Write an informative essay.

- Think about your purpose and audience.
- Begin with an introduction that states your topic and tells why it is important.
- Write information about your topic in the body of the essay. Be sure to use facts, definitions, and details.
- End with a conclusion that wraps up the essay in an interesting way.
- Include an illustration about your topic.

Start here ▶

LANGUAGE ARTS PURPLE

LANGUAGE ARTS PURPLE

Simple Subjects
Find Simple Subjects

Read the sentence and underline the simple subject.

1. The little boy threw a snowball.

2. Strong and cold winds blew from the north.

3. The stores in this town close at eight o'clock.

4. Two brown deer with bushy white tails jumped into our yard.

5. Jane skipped along the wide sidewalk by the park.

6. The happy puppy curled up on the soft bed.

Write a sentence of your own. Then, circle the simple subject of your sentence.

7. _____

_____

_____

Revise Your Informative Essay
Revise with a Checklist

Follow this checklist as you revise the draft of your informative essay. Check off each box after you complete each item.

☐ Check that the essay's topic is clear.

☐ Include an introduction, body, and conclusion.

☐ Use facts, definitions, and details to explain the topic.

☐ Check that no important ideas or details have been left out of the essay.

☐ Put all ideas and details in the correct order in the essay.

☐ Add linking words and phrases to connect ideas.

☐ Remove ideas and details that are unimportant or unnecessary.

☐ Simplify or shorten sentences that are too long.

Unit Review and Proofread Your Informative Essay
Proofread with a Checklist

Follow this checklist as you proofread the draft of your informative essay. Check off each box after you complete each item.

WRITING SKILLS

- [ ] Begin each proper noun with a capital letter.

- [ ] Begin each sentence with a capital letter.

- [ ] Use commas correctly in compound sentences.

- [ ] Fix sentence fragments. You may need to add a subject or predicate.

- [ ] Spell all plural nouns correctly.

- [ ] Spell all possessive nouns correctly, and check that all apostrophes are in the right place.

- [ ] Check the spelling of words you are unsure of in a print or online dictionary.

Unit Checkpoint and Publish Your Informative Essay

Publish Your Informative Essay

Write the final copy of your informative essay in your best handwriting. Write a title for your essay on the first line.

_____

_____

_____

_____

_____

_____

_____

_____

_____

WRITING SKILLS

_____

_____

_____

_____

_____

_____

_____

_____

_____

_____

_____

_____

_____

LANGUAGE ARTS PURPLE

Being Verbs and Model Persuasive Essay

Model Persuasive Essay

Use Johnny's persuasive essay as you work through the lessons in this unit.

title ⟶ **Tennis, Anyone?**

Cedar Park is a nice place. It has a pond and lots of grass. There are swings, jungle gyms, soccer fields, and basketball courts. There is a lot to do in Cedar Park. Yet Cedar Park does not have a tennis court. This must change. The city should build a

opinion ⟶ tennis court in Cedar Park.

— introduction

Cedar Park should have a tennis court because playing tennis is fun. It is a great way to stay in shape, too. Also, Cedar Park is the only park with room for a tennis court. A tennis court would fit perfectly on the patch of grass behind the soccer fields. In addition, Cedar Park is a good place for a tennis court because it is in the middle of town. People can take a bus or walk to Cedar Park.

supporting reasons: facts, opinions

— body

The city should build a tennis court in Cedar Park because tennis is a great sport. The park has room for a court, and the park is easy to get to. Cedar Park is already good, but a tennis court would make it great!

— conclusion

LANGUAGE ARTS PURPLE

Being Verbs and Model Persuasive Essay
Respond to the Model Persuasive Essay

Answer the questions about Johnny's persuasive essay.

1. What opinion does Johnny have about Cedar Park?

   _____

2. What is the first paragraph of Johnny's persuasive essay called?

   _____

3. In what part of the essay does Johnny give the reasons for his opinion?

   _____

4. What is one fact that Johnny gives to support his opinion?

   _____

   _____

   _____

5. What is one of Johnny's reasons that is an opinion backed up by a fact?

   _____

   _____

6. Describe the tone of the essay.

   _____

7. What are some linking words that Johnny uses?

_____

_____

8. Which linking word is used often in the essay to connect an opinion with a reason?

_____

9. What supporting reason do you think is most convincing? Why?

_____

_____

Helping Verbs & Verb Phrases and Brainstorm Topics

Brainstorm Topics

First, read the assignment for writing your persuasive essay. Then, brainstorm your topic, listing as many possible topics as you can think of.

Write a persuasive essay about a way to improve your city, town, or neighborhood.

- Think about who your audience will be.
- Begin with an introduction that states your opinion.
- Write reasons to support your opinion in the body of the essay.
- Use linking words to connect opinions and reasons.
- Choose words and phrases for effect.
- End with a conclusion that restates your opinion and reasons in a different way.

_____   _____

_____   _____

_____   _____

_____   _____

_____   _____

_____   _____

Simple Predicates and Choose a Topic
Choose Your Topic

Answer the questions to choose a topic for your persuasive essay.

1. Which topic on your brainstorming list do you care most about?

   _____

   _____

2. Which topic is a good one for a persuasive essay about improving your community? Remember, it can't be a topic that everyone already agrees on.

   _____

   _____

3. Whom do you want to convince about each of your possible topics?

   _____

   _____

Look at your answers to the questions. Choose the topic you want most to write about. Also, choose your audience for your persuasive essay.

Topic: _____

Audience: _____

Verb Phrases and Fact or Opinion

Brainstorm Reasons to Support Your Position

Write the topic for your persuasive essay. List reasons that support your opinion. Next to each reason, write an *F* if the reason is a fact or an *O* if the reason is an opinion.

My topic is _____

Reasons	Fact or Opinion
_____	_____
_____	_____
_____	_____
_____	_____
_____	_____
_____	_____
_____	_____
_____	_____
_____	_____

Inverted Sentence Order and Support Your Opinion

Gather and Organize Your Ideas

Complete the graphic organizer to plan your persuasive essay.

Topic _____

My Opinion About the Topic

Reason 1

Reason 2

Reason 3

Why Readers Should Agree With Me

Draft Your Persuasive Essay
Write Your Draft

**Read the assignment. Use your graphic organizer to help you write
the first draft of your persuasive essay. Write only on the white rows.
You will use the purple rows for revisions later.**

WRITING SKILLS

Write a persuasive essay about a way to improve your city, town,
or neighborhood.

- Think about who your audience will be.
- Begin with an introduction that states your opinion.
- Write reasons to support your opinion in the body of the essay.
- Use linking words to connect opinions and reasons.
- Choose words and phrases for effect.
- End with a conclusion that restates your opinion and reasons
  in a different way.

Start here ▶

LANGUAGE ARTS PURPLE

Unit Checkpoint and Draft Your Persuasive Essay

Tell Me About My Essay

Have another person read your persuasive essay and answer the questions.

1. What is the opinion in the essay?

   _____

2. What supporting reason makes you **most** likely to agree?

   _____

3. What supporting reason makes you **least** likely to agree?

   _____

4. Does the conclusion clearly restate the opinion?

   _____

5. Does the writer convince you that his or her opinion is correct? If so, how?

   _____

   _____

   _____

   _____

Inside Address and Revise Your Persuasive Essay

Revise with a Checklist

Follow this checklist as you revise your essay. Check each box after you complete each item.

- ☐ Check that the essay's purpose is clear.

- ☐ Check that the tone and word choice fit the audience.

- ☐ Use stronger words to describe your opinion if your opinion is not clear.

- ☐ Include an introduction, body, and conclusion.

- ☐ Use three supporting reasons in the body of the essay.

- ☐ Strengthen supporting reasons with more detail.

- ☐ Look for sentences that can be combined.

- ☐ Delete unnecessary details.

WRITING SKILLS

Address an Envelope to a Business

Address a Business Envelope

Address this envelope. Write your name and return address in the upper left corner. Write the name, company name, and address of the person to whom you are writing in the center of the envelope.

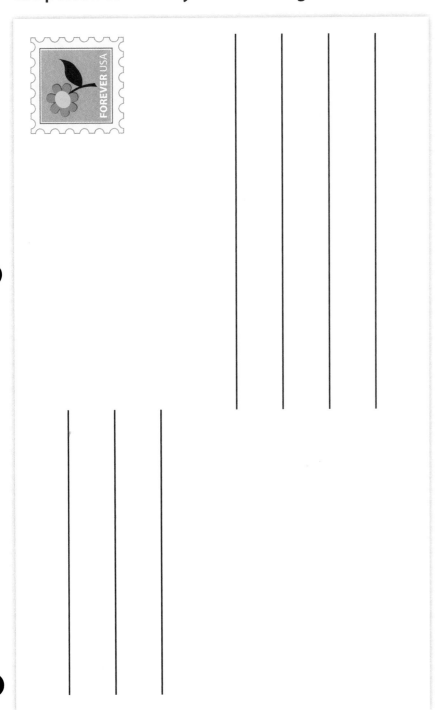

Unit Review and Turn Your Essay into a Business Letter

Model Business Letter

Use this model to help you turn your persuasive essay into a business letter.

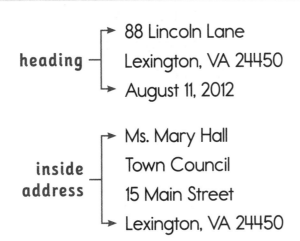

heading
88 Lincoln Lane
Lexington, VA 24450
August 11, 2012

inside address
Ms. Mary Hall
Town Council
15 Main Street
Lexington, VA 24450

salutation → Dear Ms. Hall:

body
Cedar Park is a nice place. It has a pond and lots of grass. There are swings, jungle gyms, soccer fields, and basketball courts. There is a lot to do in Cedar Park. Yet Cedar Park does not have a tennis court. This must change. The city should build a tennis court in Cedar Park.

Cedar Park should have a tennis court because playing tennis is fun. It is a great way to stay in shape, too. Also, Cedar Park is the only park with room for a tennis court. A tennis court would fit perfectly on the patch of grass behind the

body —

soccer fields. In addition, Cedar Park is a good place for a tennis court because it is in the middle of town. People can take a bus or walk to Cedar Park.

The city should build a tennis court in Cedar Park because tennis is a great sport. The park has room for a court, and the park is easy to get to. Cedar Park is already good, but a tennis court would make it great!

closing ⟶ Sincerely,

signature —
Johnny

Johnny

Unit Checkpoint and Proofread Your Letter & Envelope

Proofread with a Checklist

Follow this checklist as you proofread the draft of your business letter. Check each box after you complete each item.

☐ Begin with a heading that includes your street address, city, state and zip code, and the date.

☐ Include an inside address with the title and full name of the person to whom you are writing, the company name, and the company address.

☐ Use capital letters and commas correctly in the heading and inside address.

☐ Use a title such as *Mr.* or *Ms.* and the last name of the person to whom you are writing in the salutation, and end with a colon.

☐ Line up all parts of your letter along the left side of the page, and separate each part by a line space.

☐ Begin each sentence with a capital letter and end with a punctuation mark.

☐ Fix sentence fragments. Add a subject or predicate, as needed.

☐ Look up the spelling of any words you don't know in the dictionary.

☐ Close your letter correctly with a final word like *Sincerely*, a comma, and both a handwritten and printed signature.

☐ Match the address on your envelope to the inside address of the letter.

WRITING SKILLS